MY FIRST BOOK
OCEAN LIFE

by Alison Howard

MY FIRST BOOK OF
OCEAN LIFE

Copyright © **ticktock Entertainment Ltd** 2008

First published in Great Britain in 2006,

Ticktock Direct Ltd, The Pantiles Chambers, 85 High Street, Tunbridge Wells, Kent, TN1 1XP

ISBN 978 1 84696 006 2 pbk

Printed in China

9 8 7 6 5 4

Picture Credits: Alamy: 81; FLPA: 11, 23, 38t. OSF: 39, 40t, 41, 61; all other images: ticktock Media Archive.

CONTENTS

Words that appear in **bold** are explained in the glossary.

MEET THE OCEAN CREATURES

The oceans of the world are full of fascinating creatures of all shapes and sizes. These include fish, mammals, crustaceans, invertebrates, birds and reptiles. There are creatures so tiny that you can hardly see them, like plankton or minute, shrimp-like krill. There are enormous creatures, like the blue whale, which is bigger than three buses standing in a row. In between is an amazing range of creatures, some so weird that it is difficult to believe they really exist.

 FISH

Fish are creatures that
live in water. They breathe using gills,
have bodies covered in scales and
move using fins. They are vertebrates
(have a backbone).

MAMMALS

Mammals are vertebrates. They have warm bodies and feed their babies on milk which the females make. Most give birth to live young.

BIRDS

Birds are vertebrates and most are excellent at flying. They lay eggs. They have wings, feathers and a light but strong skeleton.

REPTILES

Reptiles are egg-laying vertebrates that have a tough skin made of scales. Most reptiles, including those that live mainly in water, lay eggs on land.

INVERTEBRATES

Invertebrates are animals which do not have a backbone. They include animals like **molluscs** and **crustaceans**, with body parts like **tentacles**, antennae, and shield-like outer coverings.

A WORLD OF OCEAN CREATURES

The map on this page shows our world.

The blue areas are oceans. The other colours show areas of land called continents. North America and Africa are continents.

Some of the creatures in this book are found in oceans all over the world, while others are only found in the oceans round specific areas.

When you read about a creature in this book, see if you can find the place where they live on the map.

Can you point to the part of the world where you live?

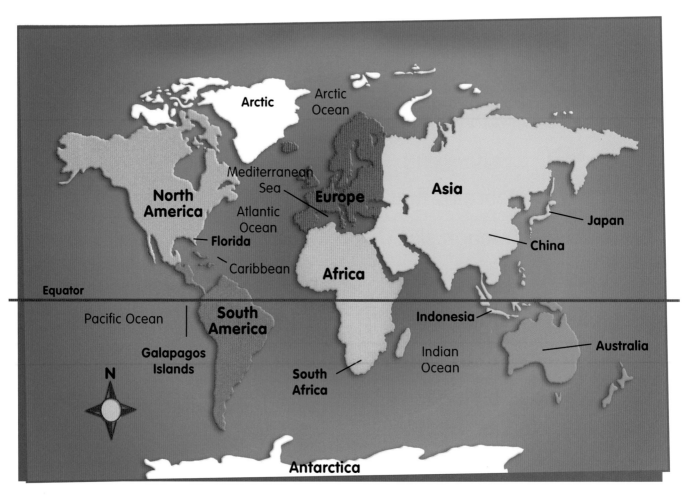

Arctic

Arctic Ocean

Mediterranean Sea

North America

Europe

Asia

Japan

Atlantic Ocean

China

Florida

Caribbean

Africa

Equator

Pacific Ocean

South America

Indonesia

Galapagos Islands

Indian Ocean

Australia

South Africa

N

Antarctica

OCEAN CREATURE HABITATS

Some creatures live right at the bottom of the ocean where only deep-sea divers can find them. In the deepest, darkest depths of the ocean, some creatures even make their own electricity to light their way. There are probably creatures hiding in the deepest parts of the ocean that have not even been discovered yet.

Some sea creatures can be seen swimming just below the waves or **basking** in the light on the surface of the water. Some creatures can jump right out of the water, or dive down deep before coming up again.

Look for these pictures in your book, and they will tell you what kind of habitat each sea creature lives in.

Tropical waters:
waters near the
Equator.

Polar regions: cold
frozen places in the
very north and south
of the Earth.

Seashore:
coastal waters
and the beach.

Seabed: the bottom of
the ocean.

Oceans

ANGLERFISH

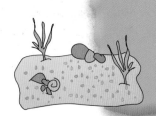

There are many different species of anglerfish around the world. The female has a long fin that looks like a fishing rod.

Anglerfish sit on the bottom of the sea and wait for their food to approach. They eat other fish.

How **BIG** is an **anglerfish?**

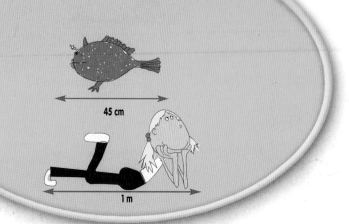

45 cm

1 m

Anglerfish eggs float up to the surface of the water where they hatch.

Soon after hatching, some male anglerfish find a female anglerfish and live on the underneath of their belly.

HATCHETFISH

Hatchetfish are found in oceans across the world, but mainly in the western Pacific. There are about 45 known **species**, and their name comes from their hatchet-shaped flat bodies.

Hatchetfish have silver sides that **reflect** light and make them almost invisible.

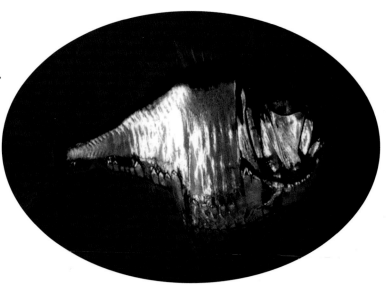

How **BIG** is a **hatchetfish?**

20 cm

1 m

Hatchetfish live at depths of between 457 metres (1,500 feet) and 610 metres (2,000 feet).

Hatchetfish feed on small fish, crustaceans and the **fry** of other fish during the day.

Light organs on the body produce a dim light that confuses **predators** and also attracts prey.

PUFFER FISH

Most puffer fish live in **tropical** and sub-tropical seas. When they feel threatened, they blow up their bodies with water so they look more frightening.

Some puffer fish have spines that lie flat against their bodies. When they puff up, these spines stick out so that **predators** find it hard to bite them.

How **BIG** is a **puffer fish?**

50 cm

1 m

Puffer fish have powerful beak-like snouts which they use to crush their food.

12

The organs of the puffer fish contain a **toxic** chemical that can be fatal if eaten.

Puffer fish feed on **molluscs, crustaceans** and coral (see page 86).

CLOWNFISH

Clownfish are brightly-coloured little fish that help the sea anemone (see page 88) to catch prey. They live in warm water.

The clownfish hides among the **tentacles** when prey comes near, and pays back the service by cleaning the anemone. The clownfish has a layer of slime on its body to protect it from the anemone's stings.

How **BIG** is a **clownfish?**

12 cm

1 m

Clownfish get their name from their bright markings that look like a clown's make-up.

Clownfish usually live in pairs within a sea anemone. They lay their eggs on rocks next to the host anemone.

STONEFISH

The stonefish lives in **tropical** waters.

It has a knobbly, patterned body that makes it look just like a stone.

This allows it to hide from **predators**.

Stonefish have deadly spines along their backs, which can inject poison into other animals.

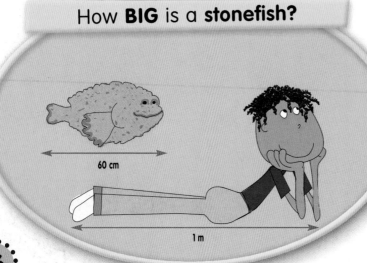

How **BIG** is a **stonefish?**

60 cm

1 m

If a stonefish is disturbed it will not swim away.
It will confront an intruder.

16

The stonefish catches shrimp and small fish in its mouth. Its spines are just used for defence.

Can you see the stonefish's eyes?

The stonefish lies on the seabed and looks just like a lump of rock – until it moves.

COELACANTH

The coelacanth is sometimes called a living fossil because it was thought to have died out 65 million years ago. It is very rare and lives in the oceans near South Africa and Indonesia.

People thought coelacanths were extinct until one was caught in 1938.

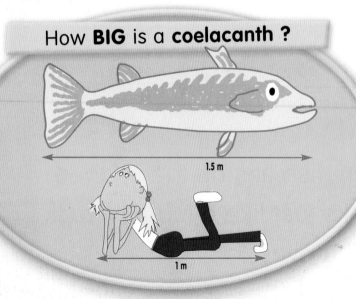

How **BIG** is a **coelacanth** ?

1.5 m

1 m

Coelacanths can open their mouths very wide, but only have teeth in the front of their mouths.

Unlike most other fish,
coelacanths give birth
to live babies.

FLOUNDER

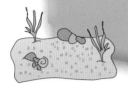 

The flounder is flat with patterned skin. It lives at the bottom of shallow waters and **estuaries** off the coast of Europe and North America.

Flounders eat small fish, squid and shrimps that live on the bottom of the ocean.

This is a winter flounder.

How **BIG** is a **flounder?**

50 cm

1 m

A flounder is covered in prickly scales and has a continuous fin that looks like a fringe round most of its body.

When flounders hatch, they look like normal fish. Gradually, their bodies flatten and their eyes move round to the same side of their bodies, just like this European flounder.

ATLANTIC SALMON

The Atlantic salmon is the best-known of many types of salmon. It is found in the northern Atlantic Ocean, but it swims up rivers to lay its eggs in shallow nests.

The female lays her eggs in winter and the male fertilises them. They hatch in the following spring.

How **BIG** is an **Atlantic salmon?**

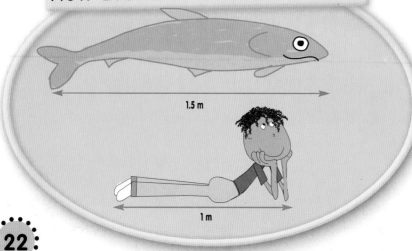

1.5 m

1 m

Salmon eat fish like herring and pilchards, squid and **crustaceans**.

Most other types of salmon, both male and female, die after laying or fertilising their eggs.

Atlantic salmon return to the sea and may breed again a few years later.

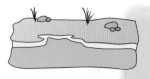

MORAY EEL

Moray eels live in coral reefs and shallow **coastal** waters of the northern Atlantic Ocean. They like to hide in crevices and launch surprise attacks on their prey.

There are about 100 **species** of moray eel. They like to eat fish and **molluscs**, like octopuses.

How **BIG** is a **moray eel?**

3 m

1 m

Moray eels have wide mouths with lots of sharp teeth, making it difficult for prey to escape once it has been caught.

Although they look like snakes, moray eels are fish.

They have very small eyes and bad eyesight, but a strong sense of smell. They use surprise to catch their prey.

BASKING SHARK

Basking sharks are found all over the world. Their name comes from the fact that they are often seen soaking up the sun at the surface near the shore.

Basking sharks eat **plankton**, small **crustaceans**, **larvae** and fish eggs.

How **BIG** is a **basking shark?**

12 m

1 m

The **gill slits** are so long, they nearly go round the whole of the shark's head.

Basking sharks' enormous mouths are filled with hundreds of tiny teeth.

They feed by moving forward in the water with their mouths wide open.

HAMMERHEAD SHARK

The hammerhead shark's name comes from its strangely shaped head, which looks just like a hammer. It is found in warm seas throughout the world.

The eyes and nostrils of the hammerhead shark are at the ends of its head. It has sharp, **serrated** teeth.

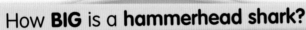

How **BIG** is a **hammerhead shark?**

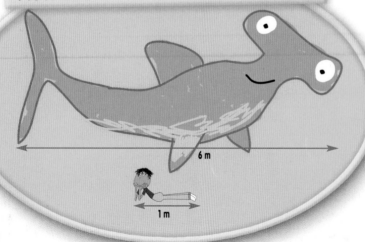

6 m

1 m

Hammerhead sharks eat squid, octopuses, rays, **crustaceans** and even other sharks.

There are five different **species** of hammerhead shark. All are extremely dangerous.

Hammerhead sharks give birth to between 20 and 40 live young, each about 70 centimetres (27 inches) long.

GREAT WHITE SHARK

The great white shark is the most dangerous fish in the sea. It lives in warm and **tropical** waters.

The great white shark has powerful jaws and rows of sharp teeth. It eats large fish, seabirds, seals and dolphins, and very rarely people.

How **BIG** is a **great white shark?**

8 m

1 m

A great white shark's teeth can each be up to 8cm (3 inches) long.

The great white shark has sharp eyesight designed to see underwater, and an excellent sense of smell – it can smell food or a tiny trace of blood from a long way away.

MANTA RAY

The manta ray is a huge fish found in warm oceans. Its name comes from the Spanish word for blanket or mantle, because of its wide, blanket-like fins.

The manta ray can leap up to 1.5 metres (5 feet) out of the water. Scientists are not quite sure why – it may do it to escape **predators** or to rid itself of skin **parasites**.

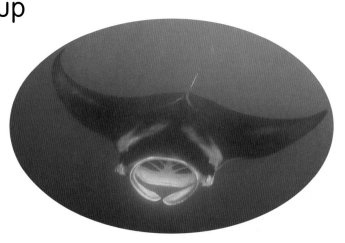

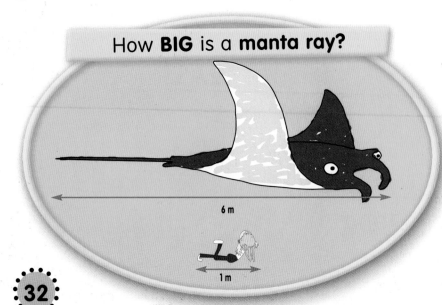

How **BIG** is a **manta ray?**

6 m

1 m

The manta is the largest of more than 300 **species** of ray.

The manta ray cruises the surface of the water gathering **plankton**, small fish and shellfish to eat. It has special scoops on the side of its head to direct food towards its mouth.

Manta rays are dark brown/black on top and white underneath.

PARROTFISH

Parrotfish live in **tropical** seas, mainly around coral reefs. They are often brightly coloured in red, green and blue, and their teeth look just like a parrot's beak.

Parrotfish use their bony beaks to scrape coral and **molluscs** and to nip off the seaweed that they feed on.

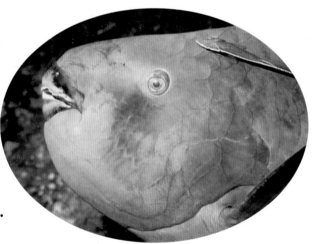

How **BIG** is a **parrotfish?**

1.5 m

1 m

Parrotfish often gather in groups to search for food.

There are many different types and sizes of parrotfish – there are 80 **species** in total.

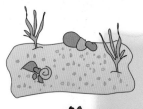

SEAHORSE

Seahorses are small, bony fish that live in warm water. Their heads are shaped like horses' heads, and they use their curly tails to cling to seaweed.

Seahorses swim very slowly, but they can change their colour to match their surroundings and hide from **predators**.

How **BIG** is a **seahorse?**

16 cm

1.2 m

Although the female produces the eggs, they are held inside the male's body until they hatch.

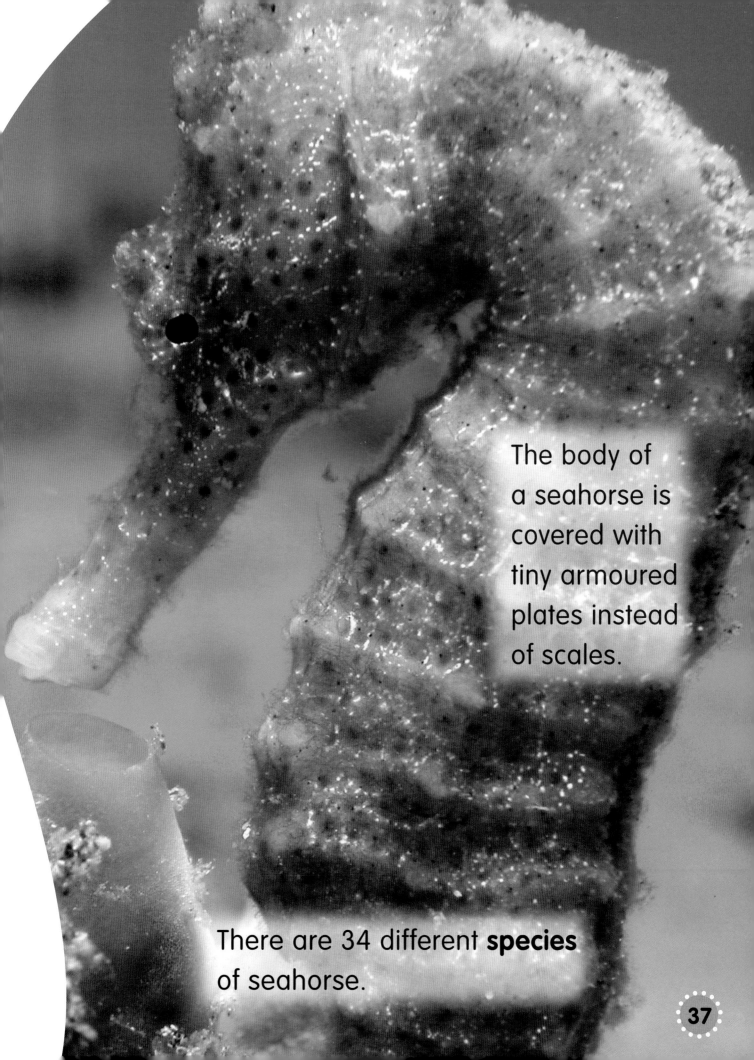

The body of a seahorse is covered with tiny armoured plates instead of scales.

There are 34 different **species** of seahorse.

FLYING FISH

Flying fish live in warm or **tropical** seas. Their name comes from their ability to leap into the air and glide as if they are flying.

Flying fish hold their fins out like wings as they leap.

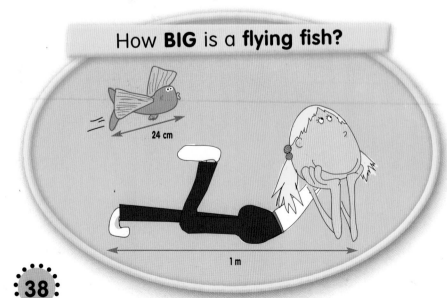

How **BIG** is a **flying fish?**

24 cm

1 m

Most flying fish glide rather than fly, but one variety actually flies for short distances.

Flying fish leap out of the water to escape from **predators**.

Before take-o͟ they quickly swi͟ to the surface at speeds of up to 55 kilometres per hour.

BLUE WHALE

The blue whale **migrates** to polar seas where there is plenty of food in the summer, and lives in warmer seas for the rest of the year. It is the largest animal in the world.

The blue whale takes in mouthfuls of water then pushes it through its **baleen** plates with its tongue. This traps **plankton**, **krill** and small fish for the whale to eat.

How **BIG** is a **blue whale?**

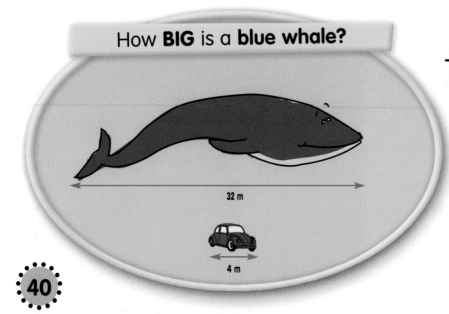

32 m

4 m

The blue whale is very rare because so many have been hunted by people.

Like other whales and human beings, blue whales breathe using lungs. They blow stale air out through a blowhole in the top of their heads.

HUMPBACK WHALE

Humpback whales are found in **coastal** waters throughout the world. People most often see humpback whales when they jump out of the water (breach).

Like other kinds of whale, humpback whales feed by sieving **plankton** and fish through **baleen** plates.

How **BIG** is a **humpback whale?**

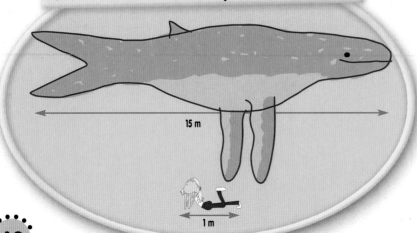

15 m

1 m

Humpback whales are grey and black, with long white flippers.

Humpback whales like to live together in a big group so they can help each other to catch food and warn each other of danger.

SPERM WHALE

The sperm whale is found in oceans all over the world, and is grey-blue with pale underparts. It has tiny flippers and large tail **flukes**.

Sperm whales have to come to the surface of the water to breathe.

How **BIG** is a **sperm whale?**

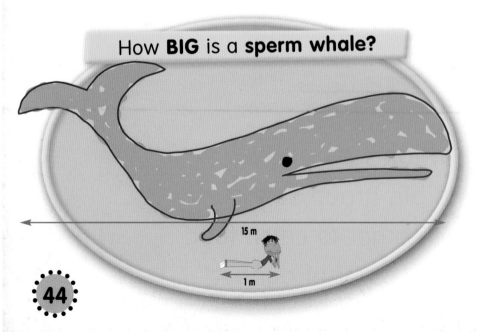

15 m

1 m

The sperm whale
has excellent
hearing and can
communicate with
other whales by
making sounds.

The sperm
whale loves to eat
octopus and squid.

It can dive to a depth of up to one kilometre
and stay underwater for more than an hour.

DOLPHIN

Dolphins are found in seas all over the world. They look like fish, but they are actually **mammals**, so they give birth to live young.

Dolphins love to eat fish. They also like to live and play together.

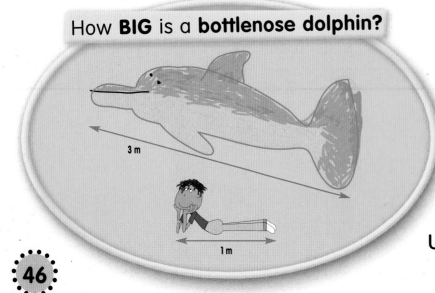

How **BIG** is a **bottlenose dolphin?**

3 m

1 m

There are 30 to 40 different dolphin **species**. The bottlenose dolphin can live up to 25 years.

Dolphins have teeth, a snout that looks like a beak, flippers and a long **dorsal** fin. They can jump high out of the water.

ORCA

The orca is found in oceans all over the world but prefers colder seas to the warmer waters near the Equator. It is also known as a killer whale.

The orca is a **mammal** and the largest type of dolphin. It gives birth to live young.

How **BIG** is a **killer whale?**

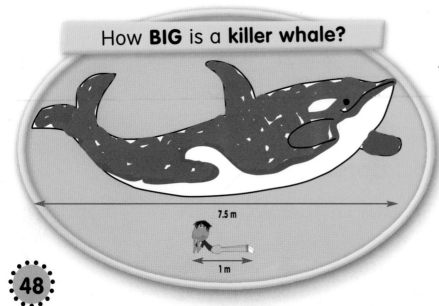

7.5 m

1 m

The orca has distinctive black and white colouring and a tall **dorsal** fin.

Like dolphins, orcas like to live in a group, called a 'pod'.

The orca eats fish, squid and seals, as well as larger animals like porpoises and small sharks.

MANATEE

Manatees are **mammals** that live near the coast and in canals near the surface of the water. North American manatees spend the winter in Florida, as they prefer the warm water.

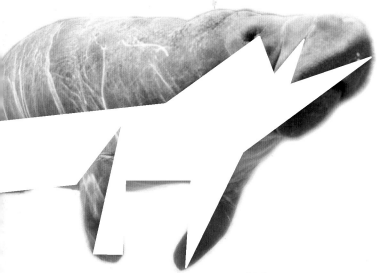

Manatees have very high nostrils so they can breathe even when most of their bodies are underwater.

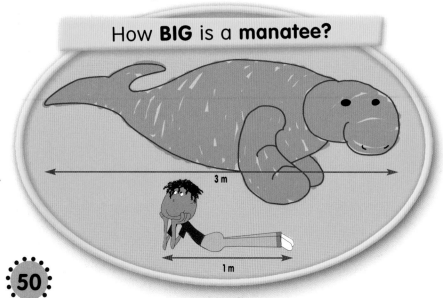

How **BIG** is a **manatee?**

3 m

1 m

They can stay underwater for about 20 minutes.

A manatee moves very slowly, using forelimbs shaped like paddles and a flat tail that helps it to swim.

Manatees spend all their lives in the water, and sleep with their nostrils poking out of the water.

SEA OTTER

The sea otter is a **marine mammal** that is related to the weasel. It lives on the coast of the northern Pacific Ocean.

Sea otters mainly eat shellfish. They sometimes use a rock to smash open the shells.

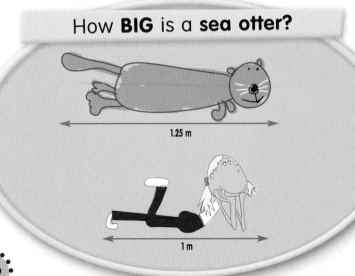

How **BIG** is a **sea otter?**

1.25 m

1 m

Unlike other **marine mammals**, the sea otter has no **blubber**. Instead, it has thick, waterproof fur.

Sea otters swim on their backs. They have up to 800 million hairs on their bodies, which help to keep them afloat.

Sea otters breed throughout the year and give birth to one pup at a time.

HARP SEAL

Harp seals have sleek bodies that are perfect for swimming. They have thick **blubber** that keeps them warm in the Arctic, where they live. They get their name from a black patch shaped like a harp on their back.

Baby harp seals have whiter fur than the adults.

How **BIG** is a **harp seal?**

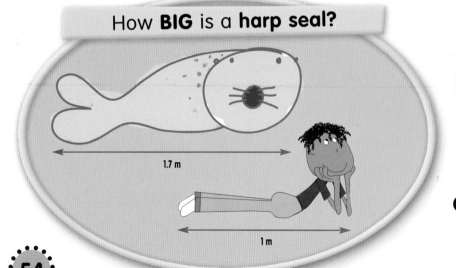

1.7 m

1 m

Harp seals catch and eat fish and **crustaceans**.

Harp seals have short, thick white-grey fur with black patches and a grey-black face.

Harp seals spend most of their lives in the water, but sometimes they go onto the ice to give birth.

WALRUS

The walrus is a large **marine mammal** that is related to the seal. It lives in the waters of the Arctic and is covered in thick **blubber** to protect it from the cold.

Walruses sleep in the water and have air-filled sacs on the sides of their necks that help to keep them afloat.

How **BIG** is a **walrus?**

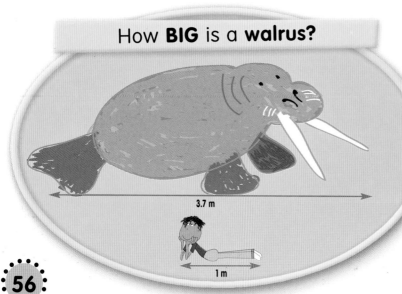

3.7 m

1 m

Walrus mothers are very protective of their pups and may adopt orphans.

The walrus has tough, wrinkled skin, large tusks and bristly whiskers that look like a moustache.

Walruses use their long, sharp tusks for digging, fighting and to show off to female walruses.

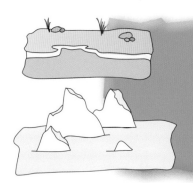

PENGUIN

Penguins are birds that are very good swimmers and can survive in extremely cold places, such as the Antarctic.

They spend most of the time in the water trying to catch fish, **krill** and squid to eat. Their wings are like flippers.

How **BIG** is an **Emperor penguin?**

1.1 m   1.2 m

Most species come on shore to breed during the warmer months, forming large colonies.

There are 17 **species** of penguin. The emperor penguin is the largest and lives in Antarctica.

Penguins are ideally suited to their environment. They have thousands of tiny feathers and a layer of fat under the skin.

BANDED SEA SNAKE

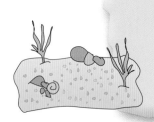

The banded sea snake lives in oceans all over the world, except the Atlantic Ocean. It is a pale shade of blue with black bands.

The banded sea snake has a tail that is shaped like an oar which helps it to swim fast.

This snake's bite is venomous.

How **BIG** is a **banded sea snake?**

75 cm

1 m

Banded sea snakes come to the surface to breathe, but they like to live on the seabed.

Banded sea snakes like to eat crabs, cuttlefish, eels, fish, fish eggs, and squid.

SALTWATER CROCODILE

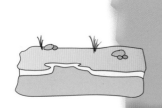

The saltwater crocodile is the largest **reptile** on the planet. Most people think crocodiles live in rivers, but these **aggressive** beasts are adapted to life in **coastal** waters of Australia, Indonesia and Asia.

How **BIG** is a **saltwater crocodile?**

6.5 m

1 m

The saltwater crocodile spends most of its life hiding in the water, waiting patiently for its next victim.

A saltwater crocodile moves with astonishing speed, dragging its victim down and tearing off large chunks of flesh.

It eats **crustaceans**, fish, turtles and birds. Sometimes it eats larger animals like buffalo.

63

GREEN TURTLE

The green turtle is a **reptile** that lives in warm Atlantic **coastal** waters. It gets its name from its green fat.

The green turtle comes to land when it wants to **bask** in the sunlight or sleep.

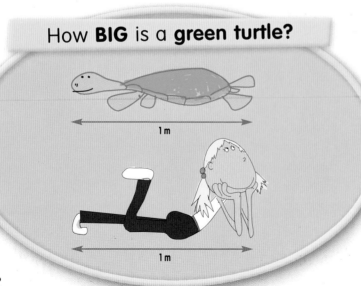

How **BIG** is a **green turtle?**

1 m

1 m

There is a major nesting area on Ascension Island in the South Atlantic.

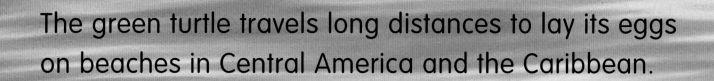

The green turtle travels long distances to lay its eggs on beaches in Central America and the Caribbean.

It can grow to about 1 metre (3 feet 3 inches) long and weigh up to 140 kg.

The green turtle lays its eggs in holes that it digs in the sand.

LEATHERBACK TURTLE

The leatherback turtle is found in oceans all over the world. It gets its name because it has no shell, just a **flexible** leathery coating of skin with ridges of bone.

Like all turtles, the leatherback turtle comes ashore to lay its eggs. When the baby turtles hatch, they scuttle to the sea.

How **BIG** is a **leatherback turtle?**

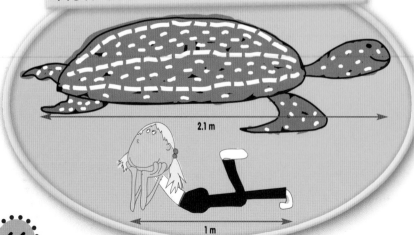

2.1 m

1 m

The leatherback turtle is the largest of all the turtles.

The leatherback turtle eats other sea creatures, and is especially fond of jellyfish.

Leatherback turtles like to swim in the open ocean.

MARINE IGUANA

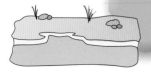

Marine iguanas, like land iguanas, are a type of lizard. They live on a group of islands called the Galapagos, which is off the west coast of Ecuador in South America.

Marine iguanas eat **algae** which grows on rocks near the shore.

They can remain underwater for up to an hour, although five to ten minutes is more usual.

How **BIG** is a **marine iguana**?

75cm

1 m

Males are more brightly coloured than females, with red and green coloured backs.

When males fight, they put their heads together and push their foe backwards. The loser has to retreat.

FIDDLER CRAB

Fiddler crabs are tiny **marine crustaceans** with one large claw. They live on and near the seashore in **tropical** regions.

Fiddler crabs make their homes by burrowing in the sand on the seashore.

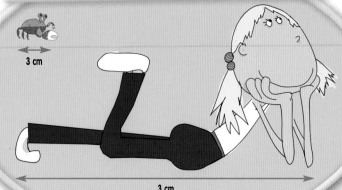

How **BIG** is a **fiddler crab**?

3 cm

3 cm

Fiddler crabs are **scavengers** that will eat anything they find on the seashore or in shallow water.

Male fiddler crabs move their large front claw in and out, just like a violinist's arm, to attract females.

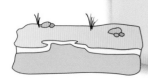

HERMIT CRAB

The soft-bodied hermit crab is found in oceans all over the world. It is so named because it hides in shells left by other creatures.

The eyes of hermit crabs are on the end of stalks that stick out of their heads.

How **BIG** is a **hermit crab?**

15 cm

1 m

Hermit crabs have ten jointed legs. The two front legs have pincers or claws.

When a hermit crab grows out of the shell it is using, it just moves to a bigger one.

Hermit crabs are **scavengers** that eat anything they can find, including plants, **plankton** and even dead sea creatures.

MANTIS SHRIMP

Mantis shrimps are small **predatory crustaceans** that live in the **coastal** waters of **tropical** and warm seas. Despite their name they are not related to shrimps.

Mantis shrimps capture their prey by hitting them with their club-like front legs and smashing them to pieces.

How **BIG** is a **mantis shrimp?**

30 cm

1 m

Mantis shrimps kill and eat fish, sometimes much larger than themselves.

Mantis shrimps can strike with the force of a bullet, and can even break safety glass in aquarium walls.

LOBSTER

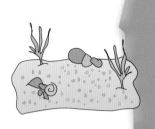

Lobsters are **marine crustaceans** which are found in oceans all over the world. They begin their lives as tiny floating organisms that make up **plankton**.

Lobsters carry on growing throughout their lives, shedding their old 'skin' as they outgrow it.

How **BIG** is a **lobster?**

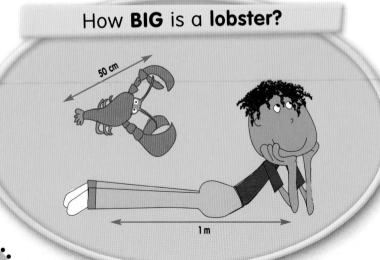

50 cm

1 m

The lobster is protected by a hard **exoskeleton** on the outside of its body.

Lobsters have five pairs of jointed legs, the first with large, pincer-like claws that are used to crush its prey.

Lobsters are **scavengers** and will eat whatever they find, but they particularly like shellfish and may attack live fish.

OCTOPUS

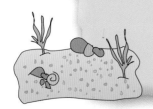

Octopuses have eight **tentacles** or arms that are covered in suckers. They use these to catch fish and **crustaceans** to eat.

There are 100 different **species** of octopuses. The largest is this giant Pacific octopus, which is five metres long.

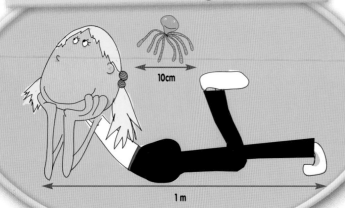

How **BIG** is a **blue-ringed octopus?**

10cm

1 m

There are two different kinds of blue-ringed octopus. Each has a **venomous** sting.

The blue-ringed octopus is found in shallow pools off the coast of Australia. When resting, it is pale brown or yellow. It only shows its blue colour when it feels threatened.

In order to escape from **predators**, octopuses squirt black, inky liquid into the water (so the **predator** cannot see) and then quickly escape.

JELLYFISH

Jellyfish live in oceans all over the world. They have soft bodies and long, stinging **venomous tentacles**, which they use to catch fish. There are 215 **species** of jellyfish.

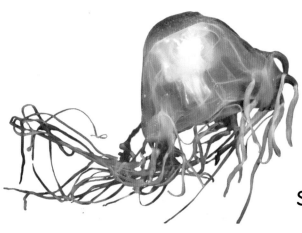

The box jellyfish is very pale blue and transparent, which makes it difficult to see even in clear water.

How **BIG** is a **box jellyfish**?

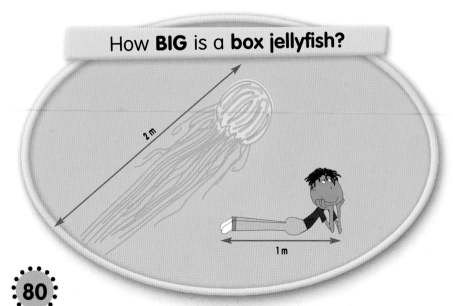

2 m

1 m

The sting of the box jellyfish is very strong, and can kill people.

This is a cannonball jellyfish.

A jellyfish's body is shaped like an upside-down bowl, and the mouth is underneath, in the centre.

SQUID

The squid is a **marine mollusc** that lives in oceans all over the world. It is closely related to the octopus.

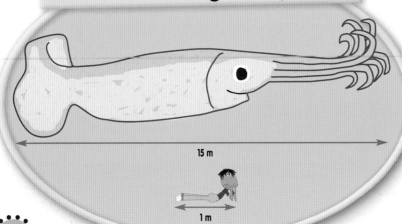

Squid eat fish, **crustaceans** and other squid. When they are angry or frightened, squid can change their colour to blend in with their surroundings.

How **BIG** is a **giant squid?**

15 m

1 m

Giant squid can reach a size of up to 15 metres (46 feet).

The squid can squirt a dark liquid called ink to make the water cloudy.

Squid have two long **tentacles** and eight shorter arms. They have a long body with two triangular fins.

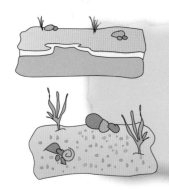

OYSTER

Oysters are **molluscs** which are highly-prized all over the world for the pearls they produce. There are many different varieties, and they are found in every ocean.

If a piece of sand enters the shell, the oyster coats it with a shiny substance called nacre to stop it scratching. This makes a pearl.

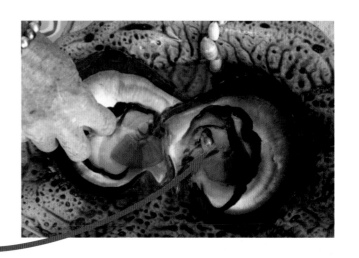

How **BIG** is an **oyster?**

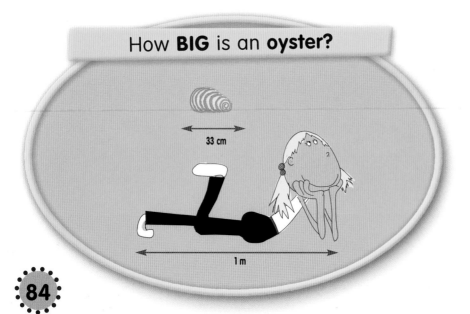

33 cm

1 m

Oyster shells are roughly oval with two halves. The shell protects the soft body of the oyster.

Oysters draw in water through their
gills, take out the oxygen to breathe
and filter out **algae** for food.

Oysters usually form
large beds, and
often attach
themselves to rocks.

CORAL

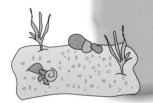

Corals are tiny **invertebrate** creatures found in oceans around the world. They come in many different colours and shapes.

Corals are tiny, soft-bodied animals called polyps. They fasten themselves to other polyps or the sea floor.

How **BIG** is a **coral?**

corals are tiny but can grow very large

1 m

As some kinds of corals grow and die, their skeletons can form large raised areas on the sea floor called reefs.

Corals eat **plankton** and tiny sea creatures. They catch them using **tentacles** that surround their mouths.

SEA ANEMONE

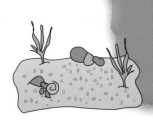

The sea anemone looks like a flower, but it is a **predatory** animal. They are found all over the world in deep oceans, **coastal** waters and shallow water, including coral reefs.

The sea anemone lives its life attached to the ocean floor, but it can move very slowly.

How **BIG** is a **sea anemone?**

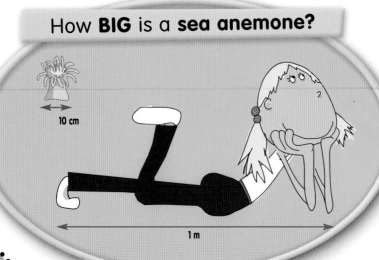

10 cm

1 m

Sea anemones eat small **crustaceans**, fish and mussels, which they sting using their venomous **tentacles**.

The body of a sea
anemone is shaped like
a **column**, with a mouth
at the top surrounded
by stinging tentacles.

There are more than 1,000
varieties of sea anemone.

SEA CUCUMBER

The sea cucumber is a cylinder-shaped **invertebrate**. It is found in oceans all over the world, from **tropical** waters to the cold depths of the deepest oceans.

They have spiny skins so that **predators** find it difficult to eat them.

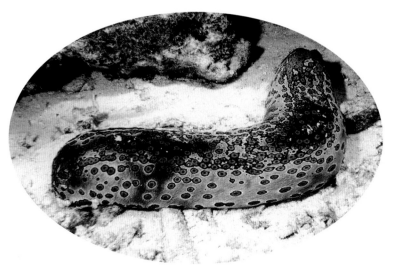

How **BIG** is a **sea cucumber?**

30 cm

1 m

Sea cucumbers eat **decaying** matter from the water or the sand at the bottom of the ocean.

Sea cucumbers have five rows of tube feet with tiny suction cups. They use these to crawl along the seabed or stick to rocks.

A sea cucumber is one of the most basic forms of life, and it does not have a brain.

The mouth of the sea cucumber is surrounded by between 8 and 30 **tentacles**.

STARFISH

Starfish are not really fish – they are **marine invertebrates**. They are found in oceans all over the world and live in shallow water near beaches.

Starfish have at least five arms or **tentacles**. They use rows of suckers on their arms to pull themselves along.

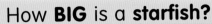
How **BIG** is a **starfish?**

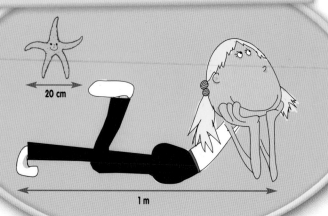

20 cm

1 m

A starfish has an **internal** skeleton made from hard bony plates called ossicles.

Starfish eat oysters and other **molluscs** from the shore and the ocean floor using their tentacles.

There are 1,500 known **species** of starfish in a wide range of sizes.

Glossary

aggressive Likely to attack or harm others.

algae Group of simple, non-flowering plants (e.g. seaweed).

baleen Horny, fringed plates that grow from the palate of some types of whale and are used to filter food from the water.

bask Lie in the warmth of the Sun.

blubber Layer of fat to protect an animal from the cold.

camouflaged A colouring which disguises an animal to help it blend in with its surroundings.

cartilage Tough, elastic tissue or gristle that forms the skeleton of some fish.

coastal Around the coast of a country or continent.

column A shape like a long cylinder.

crustacean An animal with jointed legs and a hard shell, including crabs, lobsters and shrimps.

decaying Rotting or disintegrating.

dorsal On the back, especially referring to fins.

estuary The wide lower part of a river where the tide flows in from the sea.

exoskeleton A hard outer covering that supports and protects an animal.

flexible Able to bend easily without breaking.

fluke A flat section of the tail of a whale.

fry A large swarm of young creatures,

especially fish.

fused United, blended or grown together.

gill slits Slits through which fish and some amphibians breathe under water.

internal On the inside.

invertebrate An animal without a backbone.

krill Tiny, shrimp-like ocean creatures that are eaten by whales and other creatures.

larva The early stage of development of many kinds of animal.

mammals Warm-bodied vertebrates that feed their babies on milk, which the females make. Most give birth to live young.

marine Relating to the sea.

migrate Travel long distances from one habitat to another, often in search of food.

mollusc An invertebrate animal with a soft, segmented body, usually protected by a shell.

parasites Organisms that live in or on other animals and feed off them.

predator An animal that hunts and kills other animals for food.

plankton Minute animals and plants that float and drift in open water and are a source of food for other marine life.

reflect Send back light like a mirror.

reptile Animals whose body temperature is controlled by their surroundings. Most lay eggs and have scaly skin.

scavenger An animal that feeds off waste and leftovers, rather than hunting itself.

serrated Something with a jagged edge; saw-like.

shoal A large group of fish that swim together.

spawn A mass of eggs, or to deposit a mass of eggs.

species A group of animals that share many features and can breed together.

tentacle A long flexible organ used for holding, feeling or moving.

temperate Mild, pleasant and without extremes, especially relating to climate.

tissue A collection of cells that make up the body material of an animal.

toxic Poisonous or caused by poison.

tropical Relating to certain hot parts of the world.

venomous Producing a poisonous fluid injected by a bite or sting.

vertebra One of the bones that makes up the spine.

Index